we were promised honey!

Sam Ward

T0021315

methuen | drama

LONDON · NEW YORK · OXFORD · NEW DELHI · SYDNEY

METHUEN DRAMA
Bloomsbury Publishing Plc
50 Bedford Square, London, WC1B 3DP, UK
1385 Broadway, New York, NY 10018, USA
29 Earlsfort Terrace, Dublin 2, Ireland

BLOOMSBURY, METHUEN DRAMA and the Methuen Drama logo are
trademarks of Bloomsbury Publishing Plc

First published in Great Britain 2022

This edition published 2022

Copyright © Sam Ward, 2022

Foreword copyright © Katie Hawthorne, 2022

Sam Ward has asserted his right under the Copyright, Designs
and Patents Act, 1988, to be identified as author of this work.

Cover design: Sam Ward

Images copyright © Mark Mindel, 2022

A catalogue record for this book is available from the British Library.

A catalog record for this book is available from the Library of Congress.

ISBN: PB: 978-1-3503-8135-3
ePDF: 978-1-3503-8137-7
ePub: 978-1-3503-8136-0

Series: Modern Plays

To find out more about our authors and books visit
www.bloomsbury.com and sign up for our newsletters.

Foreword

There are four warnings in *we were promised honey!*

This story will end badly, Sam says. It *always* ends badly. Are you sure you want to hear it?

So far, every time that *honey* has been performed, the audience has looked tragedy in the eye and said, yes. Tell us how the story goes.

There's a deliciousness in being warned but doing it anyway. It feels brave, thrilling even, to rise to the challenge. Or maybe we're ghoulishly fascinated by the prospect of disaster, excited to shiver in horror at the next turn of the screw. Either way, we say yes. Sam's deceptively simple question is one of theatre's oldest magic tricks: it turns the audience into conspirators, twisted together by a shared fate.

* * * *

we were promised honey! is a play about knowledge and what we do with it. From the start, the spectre of a foregone conclusion hangs in the wings, waiting to meet us in the final act. It toys with the mechanics of storytelling, knotting together dozens of possible plotlines and experimenting with how the inevitable can be suspended – even if only for a moment.

There is a bravery that runs through YESYESNONO's work, and it culminates in honey. Sam has a way of asking questions – gentle, firm, unafraid – that has become a truly powerful force, and in *honey* it is the star of the show, the full spectacle. The stage is sparse, populated only by stories, and it compresses the experience: *honey* is as large as your imagination, and the theatre becomes a lighthouse, a rocket, a golf course, a cliff edge at the end of history. The scale is dizzying, so Sam keeps checking: are you sure you want to continue?

Reading this text gives a certain advantage, of course. You don't need to wait for sixty minutes in the dark to find out how this story ends. You could turn to the last page right now! No one's going to stop you. You could work backwards, check for jump scares. Decide for yourself if the promised destination is worth the journey.

* * *

This year at the Edinburgh Festival Fringe, where *we were promised honey!* was first performed, there was a cohort of performances about looming disasters. Many of these shows asked us to imagine climate catastrophe, societal collapse, nuclear apocalypse: each fate easily rationalised as the logical conclusion to a world driven by human greed. The first full Fringe in three years, since COVID-19 changed our lives, it was little wonder that artists wanted to talk about dystopian near-futures. We all needed catharsis. But although *honey* shared its fascination with the future with several other plays, it stood apart in the way that it puts the future on stage. In this play, the future isn't a fixed point, but something mutable. When you think of the future, is it tomorrow? Or next week? Or five hundred years from now?

Rather than solemnly marching its audience towards a final destination, *honey* simply collapses time and space. The many stories in this play are not linear; they thread through each other like fables, spread into the future like rumours. Every time that Sam looks to the future he splinters the audience into shards of possibility. We're the protagonists, alongside atoms and skyscrapers and new-borns, and with every prophecy, dispensed with the jaunty yet cryptic tone of a tabloid horoscope, there is the option to claim it – to think, maybe that one's about me.

For a play that is about fate, *honey* is also deeply concerned with choice. From the very beginning, we know that this is a situation in which there are decisions to be made. That although the ending is fixed, the path towards it is negotiable.

This careful handling of the audience, equipping us with boundaries but leaving just enough slack for surprises, is now a YESYESNONO trademark. Earlier plays like *[insert slogan here]* and *Five Encounters on a Site Called Craigslist* established an ethos of care, and a practice of taking the audience extremely seriously. In *honey*, this ability to build trust is put to the test, used to ask needle-sharp questions about what we see when we look straight ahead.

This trust allows us to admit that it is both terrifying and oddly comforting to think that our fates might already be sealed – and how it is equally terrifying and hopeful to think that we have room to bargain. Who's at the wheel? Can we start again? Or is this just the way it is?

* *

Questions like these are the bedrock of tragedy. In Sophocles' *Oedipus Rex*, possibly the most enduring Ancient Greek tragedy of all, knowledge of the future is a curse. In that play there is a plague, and Oedipus commands a seer named Tiresias to reveal the source of the sickness. Tiresias refuses to speak but Oedipus demands it, insistent on hearing the truth. Tiresias miserably confesses that Oedipus himself is to blame, the consequence of a prophecy made at his birth that, unknowingly, he would murder his father and marry his mother.

Two thousand years later, humans have told this story so many times that Oedipus is the butt of a joke, a throwaway Freudian punchline. But sometimes we omit how Oedipus, after hearing the truth, decided to ignore it – and how Tiresias was blamed for the very events that he foretold. That despite it all, there was always a choice to be made.

These figures are tropes now. The tragic protagonist who fails to outrun fate, and the prophet cursed by the ability to see how everything ends. We meet them time and again, in fiction and in our reality. Rarely does anybody truly want to hear bad news, and certainly nobody wants to be the messenger.

It comes as a relief when *we were promised honey!* upends this dynamic, partly because – spoiler! – there isn't really an ending at all. There are some devastating, world-ending explosions. But some of the endings in this play feel more like beginnings, and some of the endings haven't even happened yet. The other endings we already knew, but maybe we tried not to think about them.

*

It's no small endeavour to fly an audience to the end of the universe and bring them home safely. But Sam knows how to land, and he does so with flair – his tone veering between the calm confidence of an A&E nurse, the bouncy earnestness of a tour guide, and the grandeur of a preacher cursed with a vision. *we were promised honey!* is a journey to the outer reaches of our imagination: it asks us to take in more than we can comprehend, and with that comes fear. But there is always the assurance that Sam is equipping us with survival skills, doing his best to prepare us for tragedy on all scales – personal, collective, planetary.

By the end, we're back at the start and the stage is ready for the next performance. But maybe we're braver than we were before.

Katie Hawthorne

31 October 2022

we were promised honey!

For Mum and Dad
One you can read, at last

we were promised honey! was first performed at Paines Plough Roundabout @ Summerhall as part of the Edinburgh Festival Fringe 2022.

It was subsequently performed at Soho Theatre, London, from 22 November to 3 December 2022.

It was commissioned by Soho Theatre and supported by New Diorama Theatre and Arts Council England.

Writer/Performer   Sam Ward
Producer   Rhian Davies
Sound Design   Carmel Smickersgill
Lighting Design   David Doyle
Additional Direction   Atri Banerjee
Dramaturgy   Deirdre McLaughlin and Craig Gilbert
Creative Collaborators   Amalia Vitale, Heloise Lowenthal and Josie Dale-Jones
Illustrations   Mark Mindel

Thank you:
Nathan Ellis, Hal Coase, Emma D'Arcy, Tom Bailey, Lou Doyle, Chris Whyte, Trevor White, Tilda O'Grady, Will Spence, Nikhil Vyas, Linda van Egmond, Jack Hilton, Clara Potter-Sweet, David Byrne, Will Young, Justin Masterson, Chris Thorpe, Adam Brace, Gill Greer, Stella Green, Emily Davis, Alvin Yu, Lamorna Ash, Daisy Moseley, Ibaad Ur Rehman Alvi, Thea Slotover, Emma Clark, PJ Stanley, Ava Wong Davies, Franky Murray Brown, Georgia Bruce, Sammy Glover, Tom Foskett-Barnes, Jonny Purkiss, Marco Alessi, Ela Portnoy, Maya Little, Safia, Joe, Seth, Linda, Laura, Faithia and Abra.

Utopia is on the horizon. I move two steps closer; it moves two steps further away. I walk another ten steps and the horizon runs ten steps further away. As much as I may walk, I'll never reach it. So what's the point of utopia? The point is this: to keep walking.

Eduardo Galeano

prologue

the

beginning

of

the

end

On August 10th 2018 Richard Russell stole an empty airplane from Seattle-Tacoma International Airport.

The empty plane he stole was a Horizon Air Bombardier Q400. And Richard Russell was twenty-nine years old.

During his hijacking Richard flew the empty plane for one hour and fifteen minutes. He executed a number of manoeuvres referred to afterwards by watching pilots as 'awesome'. He said he'd learnt how to do them from video games.

During the entire time of his hijacking Richard had an extended conversation with air traffic control.

That's the conversation that we're hearing now.

Richard Russell grew up in Wasilla Alaska, having moved there when he was seven. After he met his wife Hannah they moved to Washington State so that Hannah could be closer to her family. During this time Richard took a job on the ground service at Horizon Airlines, which meant he covered baggage handling.

Richard had been studying for a Bachelor's in Social Sciences. He wanted to use his Bachelor's degree to become a pilot. Or to join the Armed Forces. Or to become part of the upper management team at Horizon Airlines. He wanted to move to Alaska with his wife and raise a family there.

And then on August 10th 2018 Richard Russell stole an empty plane from Seattle airport.

And when they asked him how he was going to come down safely he said he hadn't really thought that far ahead.

The show that we're about to do is a story about the future
The story that we're going to tell is a story about us
The story of our future

It's a story that we are going to tell together
I hope that sounds okay.

My name is Sam. I wrote this show.
The bits that are written anyway
This bit for example, that I'm saying right now

And as the writer of the show I want to tell you now that the
story that we're going to tell, the story of our future
Doesn't have a happy ending.
It is not a story that is going to end well for us.

Now, I appreciate that might be a bit of a bummer.
You might think that it's a bit of a shame to tell a story, in
these times, about us crashing towards some inevitable
unhappy end.

Unfortunately that's just the way the story goes. I'm sure we
could list the reasons why.
Nuclear war
Climate change
Rampant disease

There's a lot, isn't there? It can be difficult to think about.

So… now that I have spoiled the ending, you have a choice
to make.
You can choose whether we start or not.
Now you know how the story ends you might want to not
start at all.
That's fine, understandable.
You might think that, rather than an unhappy ending, it
would be better instead, to just sit here in silence until the
end of the advertised running time, which will be about an
hour.

An hour of silence.

So maybe you do want to start. We can do that.
Even though I've told you how the story ends, you might

want to start anyway, just to see what happens.
So here's what we'll do
If this audience would like to start their story then we will
need one member of this audience to simply say the words
out loud in this space:
'I would like to begin'.
And only then will the story begin.

We wait for an audience member to speak.
And eventually they do.
And when they do.

Okay.
Well.
If that's what you want. –

The story will begin in the room that we're sat in right now
Which is to say [name of theatre] on the [date].
This story will begin with the people that are here right now.
It will begin with all of you.
Sat where you're sat right now.
Doing the things that you're doing.
Which is to say
Sitting, listening to me talk
Or trying to figure out the quietest way to eat some crisps
Or taking off your shoes which you're allowed to do by the
way.

And whilst we're here doing all that, one of you is going
to speak.
I don't know who it's going to be.

Chooses and approaches a random audience member.

All I know is that in a few seconds a completely random
member of this audience will say the words:
'How much longer is this going to go on for?'

How much longer is this going to go on for?

We wait for an audience member to speak.
And when they do:

And Sam, that's me, will say:
'I'm sorry?'
And that same audience member will repeat themselves
and say:

'I said, how much longer is this going to go on for?'

How much longer is this going to go on for?

And I'll say: 'Well we haven't really started yet. This is just
the prologue.'

And that audience member is going to sigh very loudly:

We wait for the audience member to sigh.
And when they do:

It's a much deeper, more exasperated sigh than that I think.

The audience member sighs deeper.

And they'll say, 'This is just the prologue?'

This is just the prologue?

Oh my god

Oh my god

Can't we get things moving?

Can't we get things moving?

I have a very busy day.

I have a very busy day.

I'm a very important person.

I'm a very important person.

And I'll say, well the prologue is sort of dramaturgically important actually. I have to set up themes that will become relevant later and sort of lay conceptual groundwork before we get to the beginning –

And you say, 'Right, well I think you've done that now.'

Right, well I think you've done that now.

And I say, 'Yeah I guess I have.'

And you say, 'Okay, so how does the story actually start?'

Okay, so how does the story actually start?

And I say, 'Okay. This is how the story actually starts. Let me get you up to speed.'

chapter

one

Two seconds after the end of this show all of you will be on your feet giving a standing ovation with cries of, 'Encore! Encore!'

Four seconds after the end of this show some of you will still be putting on your shoes.

Three minutes after the end of this show one of you will still be in your seat staring thoughtfully at the stage, hoping that somebody on the other side will notice you and think, 'Look how deep in thought that person is; I bet they're having interesting thoughts.'

Four minutes after the end, two members of this audience will start a conversation about their mutual love of bumblebees and during their discussion of pollination cycles they will find that they are standing closer than they were before.

Five minutes after the end of this show one of you will check the news app on your phone, close it, and then immediately open it to check it again.

Ten minutes after the end of this show someone here will finally receive a reply from the exact person you want to receive a reply from – you know who it is – and will spend the next twenty minutes agonising over a response that will eventually read: 'Haha. So true!'

Thirty minutes after the end of this show some of you will be sat in the next show, enjoying it much more than this show because that show will have a live shark in a tank and this show doesn't have any fish at all.

Some of you are hungry right now, hands up who's hungry?

Audience members raise their hands.

What's your favourite thing to eat?

The audience member answers.

In one hour you will find the most delicious [food] there is in this city and it will taste so good that for the first time in your life you will actually write a review on Yelp.

Who's got work they've got to do today?

Audience members raise their hands.

One week after the end of this show you'll send an email that reads: 'Thanks Claire. This is great,' before standing up and going to your manager's office and telling them you're moving to an abandoned island in the sea.

Who here's a bit hungover?

Audience members raise their hands.

I have no idea what's going to happen to you lot I just wanted to know where the legends were.

One year after the end of this show one of you will decide to go back to university to study archaeology.

In five years one of you will leave your church and get really into cryptocurrency.

In ten years one of you will start learning to code so you can invent an app which will make you a billionaire.

While someone else will stop learning to code so you can start a farm and raise chickens there.

In thirty years one of you will become an MP.

In forty years one of you will wake up one morning filled with the divine revelation that you are the Christ.

And in fifty years one of you will help a stranger out whilst on holiday.
So who's it going to be? Hands up. Who's a helpful person, good in a stressful situation?

Audience members put up their hands

What's your name?

The audience member answers.

Where do you want to go on holiday, [name]?

The audience member answers.

Our story starts in fifty years, [name], with you in [location], [name], having an absolutely lovely time.

What do you like to do when you're on holiday?

The audience member answers.

That's exactly what you're going to be doing, [name]. In fifty years you will be [activity]. You'll be having such a good time that at first you won't notice when someone approaches you looking sort of scared like something huge is happening to them but then they'll tap you on the shoulder and they'll say:

'Excuse me. I'm sorry to interrupt. But I think I'm having my baby and I don't have anyone to help.'

And you'll say: 'Oh my god. Um. Okay. I can help. Let's get you to a hospital.'

Do you drive, [name]?

The audience member answers.

Well in fifty years you will have learnt. / That's good. So in fifty years you will be driving a person who is giving birth to a living child in your car down a motorway which is absolutely packed with cars.

It will be car after car after a car, a car sandwich, a sea of cars. Are you an angry driver, [name]?

The audience member answers.

That's good. That's exactly the right attitude you'll need to have.

The person that you're helping will say: 'Can we go any faster? This baby isn't going to wait!' and you'll say, 'Don't worry, I think I know a shortcut' and you'll take a slip-road off the motorway down an empty road.

Do you have a good sense of direction, [name]?

The audience member answers.

Depending on your sense of direction it will either take you a short time or a worryingly long time to realise that you have absolutely no idea where you are. You will find yourself, [name], in the middle of the woods, tall trees blocking out the sun, nobody else around and this will be, [name] exactly where your car decides to break down.

So in fifty years you will find yourself walking through a dark, pine forest, [name], no idea where you are, holding the hand of somebody about to give birth. The forest will feel so vast, as if it goes on forever. It will be so dark that you'll feel the other person stop and they'll say: 'We have to stop. We are completely lost! What are we going to do?' and for a moment, [name] you won't have anything to say. You're going to be in the dark in the middle of the woods with no idea where to go, no phone signal and then …

In the distance you'll see a light; like a beacon flashing on and off. And you'll say: 'You see that light? That's where we've got to go; we'll find help there.'

So you'll get yourself together, [name], as you always do, and you'll say: 'I think I know how to make a splint. I think I watched a Bear Grylls episode where he made a splint.' And the person you're carrying will say: 'Did you see the episode where he makes a racquet out of twigs and sets a cave on fire and then uses the tennis racquet to literally hit bats out of the cave like he's playing badminton?'

Have you seen that episode, [name]?

The audience member answers.

Good, so you'll have common ground. / Watch it before this, okay, so you've got something to talk about. So using your Bear Grylls racquet, bat-fire navigation skills you'll follow that light through the dark, tall trees, until finally you'll reach the end of the woods. And when you reach the end of the woods you'll realise that the woods are in fact on a cliff and the light that you've been following is in fact the light of a lighthouse on that cliff, looking out over the sea.

So you'll say: 'Wow! Who knew there was a lighthouse here!' and you'll start to make your way towards the door but you'll feel the other person stop and you'll turn and you'll see that they've fallen, badly, on their ankle, and they can't get up. And they'll say: 'I can't keep going, this is the end. I'll just have the baby here.' Are you a strong person, [name]?

The audience member answers.

That's right, I get that feeling from you. / I don't think that's right; I think you are. You'll look at this person on the ground and you'll look at the lighthouse and back at them and the gap between and you'll say, 'Get on my back, I'm going to carry you there.'

Now, some of you might wonder whether that's even possible. Some of you might doubt that [name] would ever be able to carry a pregnant person on their back across all that way. But I promise you that in fifty years, [name] will find a strength they didn't know they had and they will pick this person up and carry them on their back from the woods across the way and to a lighthouse door, where they will bang their fist and ask to be let in.

And when the lighthouse keeper opens the door he'll take one look at you, one look at the person on your back and say: 'Let's get you upstairs.'

So the three of you will make your way up the spiral staircase in the middle of the room, up to the top floor, the room where the bulb is. And you'll lay this person out on blankets and cushions and you'll say: 'Okay. Here we are. Over to you.'

So using nothing but your hands and a manual on dolphin pregnancies you will have found in a cupboard downstairs, you will help this person you carried on your back give birth, right there in your arms.

In fifty years you will be holding a brand new human being, [name]. A little thing that you will stand up to support with your arm like this.

And as you do that, [name], you're going to look out the window of the lighthouse. From up here you'll be able to see the world all around. You'll be able to see the woods that you came through, you'll be able to see the wall to wall traffic in the distance, you'll be able to see the [activity], you'll be able to see back, right back to the trip you took to get here, back to the day that you decided to go on holiday, all the way back, right back, to the moment that you heard these words in this theatre all those years ago.

And you'll remember someone telling you, [name], that your story could only end one way. And for reasons that you don't completely understand you'll look down at this little baby, completely new to the world, and you'll say:

'By the time you're grown, this world will be a better place for you to be.'

And when you say those words in the top floor of a lighthouse in fifty years, they will feel very true.

And that's what happens fifty years after the end of this show.

Richard's voice returns, talking to ground control. We listen for a moment.

Once Tacoma ground control worked out what was happening on the 10th August 2018, their first priority was to try and get Richard Russell to come down.

You can imagine what their first thoughts must have been when they realised what had happened. You can imagine the sort of things that must have gone through their head.

But when they made contact with the hijacked plane, Richard told them that he didn't want to hurt anyone. He asked them specifically to keep him away from any incoming planes. He apologised for ruining their day.

To help with the landing, ground control brought a pilot onto the call. The pilot asked Richard if he knew how to put down the landing gear. Richard told him that he did.

'You think if I land this successfully,' Richard asked, 'Alaska will give me a job as a he pilot?'

'You know, I think they would give you a job doing just about anything if you can pull this off,' the pilot replied.

Ground control pointed out McChord Field to Richard, a space big enough for an untrained pilot like him to try and land his plane. McChord Field is a US Air Force base out in Seattle, with around 7,200 personnel.'

'Why don't you try and land there, Rich?' they said

But Richard didn't try and land.

'This is probably jail time for life isn't it?' said Richard. 'I mean I would hope it is for a guy like me.'

Now, obviously we have no way of knowing the minutiae of what really happened up there in that plane, the thoughts that were going through Richard's head ...

But I like to imagine, when I tell the story, that it was in that moment, as Richard circled McChord Field ... that he tuned his radio to a station somewhere below, found a song to which he knew most of the words, turned his plane towards the Olympic Mountains in the distance...and chose to keep flying, just a little longer, just while that song continued to play.

Richard's voice fades.

We have now started our story. That was the start.
Went well, I thought.
Thank you, [name], I thought you were very interesting.

Now we decide if we want to keep going.
We don't have to ... but we can.
If this audience wanted to continue with their story, then we will need one person in this audience to volunteer to help tell the next chapter
Which that person would do simply by by raising their hand
And saying:

'I would like to know what happens next'

And only then will we keep going and find out.

We wait.
And eventually an audience member raises their hand and says:

I would like to know what happens next.

What's your name?

The audience member answers.

At some point in the next chapter, [name] I'm going to ask you to come up and join me onstage.

It's not going to be scary, it's not going to be weird, I just want you to be ready for it.

Okay.
Here's what happens in our story next, [name].
Let me get you up to speed.

chapter

two

Over the next decades, [name], the world is going to drastically change. Towers made of glass will appear in the desert. Wires will be laid under the sea. Refrigeration tech will exponentially improve.

Fifty years after the end of this show someone here will be watching the anniversary production of the shark tank show, still performing with the original cast.

Someone else will just be finishing their 15,000th Yelp review.

In sixty years' time two people who met in this theatre will be sat on a sofa watching another documentary about bees, and when one turns to the other and says, 'Can you pass the remote?' the other will say back, 'I don't love you anymore,' get up, pack their bags and leave to become an architect.

In seventy years, after posting 237 videos explaining why they are the Christ, someone here will check their DMs to find two people asking if there's an application form to become disciples.

In eighty years one of you will open the news app on your phone, close it, then leave your house in the night holding a sharp axe in your left hand.

Ninety years after the end of this show a baby born in a lighthouse will be going to school for the first time.

And in one hundred years you, [name], will be sat in an office somewhere far away from where we are now.
The office will be in a block of offices inside a tower in the middle of a desert valley.
[name] will be sat in an office at the top.
[name] is the only one of us who will, in one hundred years' time, have done the requisite things one needs to do to sit in the top office of a tower block like this. If you are the sort of person who measures success in 'height of office relative

to other offices' then [name] will be probably the most successful person you'll ever know.

As the CEO of a global company, [name], it's only right that you have the biggest office in the space. Your office, [name], will be built in the exact same spot that a lighthouse used to be. You'll know that, [name], because of the great round walls made out of glass.

Breathe in for me, [name].

In one hundred years' time you will be sat in this office waiting for a signal to go downstairs and introduce the world to the most important revolution since the internet.

Breathe out.

Breathe in for me, [name]

You believe that PARADISE, the beta version, the one that you're about to show, will revolutionise the course of human history forever.

Breathe out.

Soon your assistant is going to come in through those doors and tell you that they're ready for you downstairs.

What's your favourite thing to drink?

The audience member answers.

In moment like these, [name], you will allow yourself a little [drink]. You'll get up from your chair and take one out of the mini-fridge set into the wall, then stand at one of your great glass windows looking down at the desert stretching out. From up here, you'll be able to see the entire crowd gathered outside.

Where do you live at the moment, [name]?

The audience member answers.

In the speech that you're about to give, [name], you will refer to [place] as the 'birthing place of PARADISE', the place where this all began.

You will remember the moment when your realtor asked if all one hundred rooms in the block needed electricity as the moment when you realised that what had originally started as an app for booking holidays had become an entire company, a brand, a global hub for cutting edge research into future tech, all of it culminating in what you're about to unveil now.

From up here you'll be able to hear the crowd ten floors downstairs. You will have made sure this event was well attended, televised.

Do you enjoy public speaking?

The audience member answers.

It's important, before making a big speech, to properly rehearse your words.

Repeat this after me, enunciate:

Paradise is ours to make.

Paradise is ours to make.

See? Doesn't that sound good? That sounds good to me, that's why we do this, that's why we rehearse.

With those words, [name], you'll tell the crowd that PARADISE isn't just a product but is the start of a new story. You'll tell the crowd that PARADISE isn't just technology, but is a new future, a new way of managing the world...

You'll tell the crowd that someone somewhere told you this story could only end one way. PARADISE will prove them wrong.

Are you ready, [name]?

The audience member answers.

Do you want to come and join me onstage?

The audience member comes down.

When your assistant comes in and tells you that they're
ready for you downstairs, you'll take the glass elevator down
ten floors. Two bodyguards will meet you at the bottom
and as you walk across the hall towards the doors you'll feel
someone press a cool bottle of water into your hand.

When you step outside you'll hear the roar of the crowd
and feel the heat of the desert against your skin.

Look right ahead of you, [name], look right where my
shoulder is.

That's where the photographers will be. Remember to allow
them time to take your photograph before you start the
speech. Give me a dignified look.

They do so.

Look at that face. That is the sort of dignity that comes with
success. That's the face that will be on the front cover of
TIME Magazine in one hundred years, having done what no
government could even dream of doing.

Take one step forward, [name], towards the crowd.

Look at the crowd. Try and make eye contact with each
individual person, make them feel like you're talking
straight to them.

Another step, right up to the podium.

These are the words of your speech, [name]. These words contain PARADISE, [name]. These words contain the future.

Take a deep breath.

Are you ready?

Take it.

As they go to take it …
Suddenly the lights disappear.
The sound of a disaster.
When it fades …

It will take you a little longer than everybody else to notice the man standing on the roof.

When you look up and see him, [name], remember to put your sunglasses on. Try and wear sunscreen if you can, start now. Your skin will thank you if you start wearing sunscreen regularly now.

It will be difficult to hear what the man on the roof is shouting down. You will be able to make out the word 'paradise' maybe. You will hear a word that sounds like 'betray'. You will hear the words 'the end, the end, the end'

Look up, [name], see if you can hear him.

He's waving now
The man up on the roof is gesticulating with his arms, slowly like a windmill

You'll watch him as he looks up to the sun
You'll watch as he lifts a can of gasoline above his head
You'll watch as he pours it over himself
He lights a match
The distance it takes for one to hit the ground
His body ignites
And turns into a ball of flame.

You might think, [name], that a man who has chosen to immolate himself does not scream as he burns.

You will realise in one hundred years' time, [name], that in fact, he does.

A pause.
Sam gets out a golf club.

Are you good at golf, [name]?

The audience member answers.

That's okay. It doesn't matter how good you are right now. Because in one hundred years you will actually be pretty good.

Top tip about golf, it's all in the hips. Let's get moving in our hips.

They start to rock their hips together, warming up.

You'll often find yourself drifting onto the golf course after stressful days like this, [name]. Golf is a useful game in that regard because it requires little in the way of heart-rate but focuses the mind.

Gives the audience member the golf club.

Hold the club down, address the ball
Soften the knees
Look out to the horizon

When you're invited onto podcasts, [name], you'll be sometimes asked how it feels to watch a man burning on top of a building that you own.

You know what you'll tell them?
You'll tell them that it feels like a fucking waste.
You'll tell them that over the course of your career you've learnt it isn't people who set themselves on fire who decide

where a story starts or how it ends.
You can't help anyone if you're just a pile of ash, you'll say.

The higher up your office gets, the more you realise that.

Look down at the ball.

It's important before you swing to know exactly where that
ball's going to land.
Focus your mind entirely on that spot.
It feels good, doesn't it?
To know that you're completely in control.

Take a deep breath
Lift the club up
And when you're ready
Swing.

The audience member swings.

Richard Russell's voice returns, speaking with ground control.
As the audience member returns to their seat we listen to him. He's
talking about performing a barrel roll.

One of the last things Richard Russell did during his flight
was perform a barrel roll.

For those who don't know, a barrel roll is an aviation
trick in which the plane turns over on both its lateral and
longitudinal axis, rolling over as it goes up like this and then
back down.

As a trick, it requires a huge amount of control. If you can't
control the aircraft you risk misjudging the distance and
smashing the plane into the ground.

Richard Russell had never flown an aircraft before this day,
apart from digitised versions on airplane simulators.

When he told ground control that he was going to try and complete a barrel roll, the controller replied: 'I don't think that's a good idea, Rich.'

There's a video you can find online of what happened next; someone filmed it on their phone. On the video, you watch as the plane lifts up to an elevation of around 5,000 feet. The sun is just beginning to set. And as the camera watches, the plane hinges over at a peak, like a rollercoaster, pausing at the height of the track.

And then you watch it come back down
And it gets faster, too fast, towards the sea, like something collapsing, something being dropped from a great height
You know, watching the video, that that plane isn't going to be able to pull up in time
You feel certain, absolutely certain as to what's going to happen next.

And then in the final moment it pulls up. The nose just scrapes the surface of the water, and he's away, over the head of whoever it was that captured the footage on their phone.

By this time two F-15 military jets had been scrambled to accompany Richard's aircraft. You can hear them on the audio, in the moments afterwards, genuinely disbelieving, laughing, that an untrained baggage handler with a BA in social sciences pulled off a trick like that.

They watched as the plane turned towards the only island close enough to land.

'I don't know' they heard him say, 'I kind of thought that was going to be it.'

Richard Russell's voice fades away.

Thank you everyone for participating in the story so far, in the ways that you have been. It is currently [time].
So far things seem to be going well.

The CEO section was fun. [name] did very well, I thought. I thought they were very charming.

But as the writer I want to remind you, at this point, that the story that we're telling
The story of us, and of our future
Still does not have a happy ending
Even in the moments that it feels like it might.

Some of us might want to stop here.
Some of us might want to keep going.
So here's what we'll do.
If this audience would like to keep going with their story, then we will need two members of this audience to volunteer to read the next chapter, which they would do simply by raising their hands and saying:
'I would like to know what happens next'
And only then will we keep going and find out.

We wait. Eventually two audience members say:

I would like to know what happens next.

They are asked their names and invited onto the stage. They stand at two microphones. When they're ready:

Okay you two.
Here's what happens in our story next.
Let me get you up to speed.

chapter

three

Over the next centuries, patterns will emerge. News presenters will use the same script over different nights. Insect populations will die, resurface, then die again.

In one hundred years someone in this room will finally give up on their archaeology degree.

Someone else will use everything they've saved in cryptocurrency to buy a pack of M&Ms.

One hundred and fifty years after the end of this show the new messiah will lead a band of followers to a mound to sing country songs and await the promised rapture up to God.

One hundred and eighty years after the end of this show a politician will lose their next election and when they're asked on television how it feels they'll say they're actually quite relieved.

Two hundred years from now a farmer will wake up, go downstairs, go outside and find that in the night someone cut the heads of all his chickens with an axe.

In two hundred and fifty years a woman born in a lighthouse by the sea will pass her astronaut exam and still won't be able to pay rent.

And in three hundred years ... two people who met in this theatre will be about to see each other again for the first time in a long time, in a ruined city.

In three hundred years' time, [name], you will work for a company called PARADISE that amongst other things sells high-end mini-fridges from a showroom buried two hundred metres underneath the ground.

Are you a careful person, [name]?

The audience member answers.

Your job, [name], in three hundred years' time, will be to watch the mini-fridges through the night. Usually, [name], at this point on shift you would take off your shoes, sit on the floor and rest your feet inside the CoolBoy 500: the most expensive mini-fridge you sell.

On this night, [name], you won't be able to sit still. Pacing up and down, you'll take a letter out your pocket to read again. In that letter will be written many words but the most important will be the ones that say: 'I'll be there. Long time no see. I can't wait.' scrawled in a handwriting you still remember after all this time.

You will be tired, [name]. You won't have slept. You will have been up all night waiting for today. When the buzzer for the intercom goes you'll find for a moment that you've forgotten how to breathe.

To the second audience member:

In three hundred years' time, you, [name], will be staring at a picture of a woman smiling with her hand on a mini-fridge. The picture will be peeling off a sign over a door into a building in a part of the city that you won't have visited in years.

Do you like the clothes you're wearing right now, [name]?

The audience member answers.

These are exactly the clothes you will be wearing in three hundred years. It will have taken you two hours to choose to wear these clothes, [name]. In three hundred years these will be the nicest clothes you own.

The heat will make your palms sweat. On the letter in your hand someone has drawn a picture of a bumblebee. When you reach out to the intercom and hear [name]'s voice you'll forget for a moment where you are.

Up above it is so hot
The sky is dull and white and red

The two of you will sit together on the floor, lit by the glow of a most-expensive mini-fridge, and this is what you'll say:

Read by the two audience members:

A: You came.

B: I came.

A: I didn't think you would.
You look nice. I like what you're wearing.

B: This? It's just something I threw on.

A: You look very dashing.

B: Thank you. Is that your work uniform?

A: No. These are just my clothes.

B: Oh.

Little pause.

A: It's been a long time.

B: I know. Long time no see.

A: Long time no see. What have you been up to?

B: I've been busy.
I'm an architect now.
I get paid a lot of money to design office blocks.
Is this a mini-fridge showroom? Do you sell mini-fridges here?

A: We sell lots of things. This is just the mini-fridge room.
Upstairs they sell ceiling fans.
It was nice of you to come.
I missed you.

B: I missed you too. That's why I'm here.

A: You look so different.

B: Do you think so?

A: Of course you do. Both of us. We're old now.
Did you recognise this building when you arrived?

B: No.

A: You see? It's all different. This building used to be a theatre. This is the exact same spot where you and I met for the first time.

B: Did we meet in a theatre? I don't remember that.

A: We went to see a play and you were in the audience.

B: That doesn't sound like me. I don't really like plays.

A: I don't think you liked this one.
Both of us had to read something onstage
Afterwards you asked me what I thought about bees.
Then we moved into our flat together.
Then you left me.

B: That's a very thorough rundown.

A: I thought it might be useful.
Can I ask you a personal question?

B: If you like.

A: Did you ever find what you were looking for?

Little pause.

B: No. Not really.
I thought I did but
I was wrong.

A: That's sad. I'm sorry.

B: It's okay.

A: I never watched the rest of that documentary.
I thought if I watched the end I wouldn't ever see you
again.

B: I wouldn't bother. The end is quite depressing, actually.

A: I've been waiting for you for such a long time.
I wrote you a letter because
I wanted to see you because
I thought that maybe we could start again.

Little pause.

B: I know it might feel like things are different
But actually they're not
If we do this
I'm just going to leave again.
Not immediately, but after a while I will.
And after I come back, I'll probably leave again
That's just the way it is.

A: Then let me pretend. Just until you go.

Little pause.

B: I'm not actually an architect.
It didn't work out in the end.
I was a gardener for a bit, when we still had those.
But now
I don't do anything.
I wake up every morning to the same red sky
I pull the curtains closed and I play video games until I
fall asleep
And then I just wake up again.

Little pause.

A: Tell me that you love me.
It doesn't have to be real; you can just imagine it. Just tell me that you love me again.

B: If that's what you want.

A: I love you.

B: I love you too.

A: Really?

B: Yes.

A: I love you too.

B: I love you so much.

And some time after that [name] stands up and says, 'Let's go home. Why don't you show me the way.'

And together they'll open the door and go up the stairs, past the room with all the ceiling fans, past a row of empty offices, past a photograph of someone somewhere playing golf.

And as they leave the building that used to be the theatre where they met for the first time and wander through a ruined city, one will ask the other if they remember being told, sometime long ago the story of a man who stole an empty airplane.

A story which began, one will say, on the 10th of August 2018, when that man stole a plane.
But which actually began before that, the other will say back, when that man took a job at the ground service with Horizon Airlines
And which actually began before that, they'll say, when that man first moved to Washington so his wife could be closer to her family
Which actually began before that when that man's family

visited Wasilla in the south of Alaska for the first time, when
he was just a boy
Which actually began before *that*, when that man looked up
into the sky and saw a plane for the first time when he was
just a baby,
Which actually began, they'll say, in the moment that man
was born.

And if that's true, they'll say, if that's true then surely the
story actually begins before that, a long time before that,
hundreds of years before that, let's say in old Alaska, when
a man called Skookum Jim was born, who discovered
gold buried underneath the earth and brought 100,000
prospectors and boomtowns to its shores
Which actually began, they'll say, before that, when a
Russian merchant sailed across the Alaskan Sea and
massacred the people he found on the other side
Which actually began when pioneer *homo sapiens* crossed a
land-bridge to Alaska 20,000 years ago
Or began when humans crossed the Sahara Desert for the
first time and spread out over the world
Or began when humans evolved from apes in the cradle of
the earth
Or with animals walking upright for the first time
It's a story, they'll say, which actually began billions and
billions of years ago…

And which ended, they'll finally remember, the way it was
always going to end.

With a plane spinning out of control
With metal smashing down into the earth
With an engine igniting as it hits the ground
A body burning in the wreckage of a crash.

And when they get home that night, the two of them will
look up Richard Russell on the internet. They'll read
articles about the plane he flew, about the people he left
behind. They'll read articles arguing it was an accident,

articles arguing that he meant to do it, articles about how it doesn't matter whether he chose or not, what matters is that he ruined a perfectly good island, they'll read articles that say everything happens for a reason, articles that say it's written in the stars, articles that say every choice we could have ever make has already been made, that say history, real history is finished, that say everything that could ever happen has already happened, that say the end has already been decided, the end is here already, that all we have to do is wait –

Then their computer will die as the power to their flat fails, so they'll sit in the dark on their own and wait for the next day to come with the next red sky and the next unbearable heat –

Because that's what happens 300 years after the end of this show.

A breath released.

It's exhausting, isn't it?

Isn't it exhausting?

I always get to this point in the story

The point where I want to say something different to what's actually written down

The point where I want to say that Richard never crashed in 2018

But instead, he kept flying, over the Olympic Mountains and beyond

I want to say that he landed successfully and became a pilot

I want to say that he moved to Alaska with his wife and had a family there

I want to pretend that things got better.

But I can't.

Because that's not how the story goes.

As much as I might pretend otherwise.

So instead I keep going with his story

Just as we keep going with ours.

Not because we think things will get better …

But because

What choice do we have but to keep going, even when we already know the end?

If anyone here would like to know how our story ends, then all you would need to do is say out loud, in this space: 'I would like to know how the story ends'

And only then would we find out.

I would like to know how the story ends.

Okay.
In that case.
Let me get you up to speed.

chapter

four

Over the next millennia the progress that once rattled from moment to moment will realise it doesn't have the same momentum anymore; it isn't the progress that it used to be.

Four hundred years after the end of this show someone will be heartbroken when Yelp ceases to exist, taking their life's work with them.

In five hundred years someone who moved to an abandoned island will leave their hut to find that Costa has opened a coffee shop on the beach outside

In seven hundred years the self-proclaimed messiah will be raptured up to heaven whilst their last disciple has a cigarette break in the loo.

In eight hundred years a shark will finally escape its tank in the middle of a show and will eat a woman in the audience before it suffocates onstage.

And in one thousand years you will be stood amongst a crowd of people looking up at an object that looks like a rocket with the words 'PARADISE Express' written from its bottom to its top.

You will watch as an astronaut who happens to be the love of your life gets onboard that ship. As it ascends into the sky, in search of new beginnings, you will try and fix the image of them waving deep into your memory, telling yourself that when they come back you want to remember exactly how it felt to watch them say goodbye.

The years will turn to decades, turn to centuries. In 1500 years the Earth's magnetic poles will flip. You will receive an electronic postcard from the outer regions of the Solar System, a picture of your somebody holding a novelty Santa hat in front of what looks like an exploding supernova with the words 'wish you were here!' underneath.

In two thousand years there will be a funeral for a famous CEO. When you see the photos on billboards high above the desert wastes you will think to yourself that they look very dignified, even as their body is blasted into space.

In three thousand years you will get a phone call from a man who sounds very far away. You will hear the words 'lost contact', you will hear the words 'unfortunate', you will hear the words 'the end the end the end.'

You will do what work you can. You will continue to survive.

In five thousand years the robot that makes mini-fridges in the factory where you work will realise that nobody is buying mini-fridges anymore and will decide to shut itself down. It will leave a message on its service screen that says: 'Thanks for a great time, gang' and after that you won't have a job.

In six thousand years you will leave your home to find the last working satellite on earth. When you arrive you'll clamber through the remains of an international space station to beam a message into the sky that says:

'I hope you're having a nice time… I was thinking that maybe after this, everything will start again. And the universe that comes after ours will find traces of us in their background radiation. They'll be able to sketch the shape of our story, and maybe things will turn out differently for them.'

And then you'll lie down in the satellite dish and wait for a reply.

In eight thousand years Krakatoa will erupt, throwing ash over half of the entire globe.

Someone here will find themselves sat on their sofa watching a documentary and will look out their window to see the sky turn black and will turn to their partner and say 'How do I always end up here?'

In ten thousand years what humans are left will watch as the Anthropocene comes to an end. Office blocks made out of glass will collapse into the sand. The last golf course will become a desert, then a tundra, then a rainforest filled with trees.

After sending a text twenty thousand years ago that said, 'Haha. So true,' someone here will receive a reply that says: 'Would you like to go for a drink sometime? No pressure lol. Sorry for the slow reply.'

In one hundred thousand years all writing will have been forgotten. New super-continents will form. Glaciers will appear again for the first time in millennia. Stonehenge and other monuments on Earth will finally erode.

A band of hunters in a metal cave will tell each other stories huddled round a roaring flame:

'There was a man called Richard Russell,' they'll say, 'who stole a plane and flew it all the way around the world. Even when he ran out of fuel he kept flying in the air and he never ever came back down.'

And when they tell that story in the light of a dying sun it will feel very true.

In eight billion years the Sun will collapse, all plants will die, the oceans will evaporate. Earth will be consumed by the final heat death of the star around which it has orbited for its entire life.

In one thousand billion years all stars will die; the entire universe will go dark.

In one thousand trillion years, dormant black holes will emerge, sucking all remaining matter into themselves.

In one trillion trillion trillion years atoms will internally collapse, all matter will disintegrate.

In one billion trillion trillion trillion years space and time will start to bend.
Time will no longer operate in the way it used to before.
Everything that has ever happened will be happening at once, as past, present, future dissolve into each other.
The first humans will appear in Africa
Factories will use steam to operate machinery
Someone somewhere is on fire on top of a tall building
A CEO just scored a hole in one.

In one billion trillion trillion trillion trillion years the PARADISE Express will be at the edge of the last black hole. The occupants will have a party on the ship, using the last bottles of booze they found beneath a secret hatch. The wine they drink will have been there for literally trillions of years, which means it will be very old, and therefore very good.

And so the final sound the universe will ever hear will be the voices of the last humans left alive singing on their ship, all together, as they float into the end.

At one billion trillion trillion trillion trillion trillion years the last Black Hole in the Universe will consume itself entirely, leaving nothing left, not empty space but the absence of space, not endless time but the absence of time. The end of space. The end of time.

The end the end the end.

epilogue

the

end

of

the

beginning

Here we are at the end of the show.

We made it! Congratulations.

Right now it is [time]. We are currently on schedule to meet the advertised running time.

The weather outside is [weather]. Which is good.

In two minutes' time all of us will go outside.

And then…

There is a long day ahead. Filled with choices for us to make.
But right now, we are here, waiting for the show to end.
Take a moment. Enjoy not having to choose anything, just for a bit.

I would like there to be music!

'Country Roads' by John Denver begins to play.

I thought this might be a nice way to end.
Most of us will know the words to this song, to the chorus at least.

Sam sings the opening lines of the chorus.

The verses are a little less well-known.

Outside there is the sun
The trees are green this time of year
Somewhere on the other side of the world somebody is waking up for the first time
And perhaps, in this theatre, an audience begins to sing.

You don't have to. It's not written in the script that you will.
Here you have the first choice.
You can decide how we end the show.

And whatever you choose, whether you choose to sing or
not
That won't just be how the show ends
But how your day begins.

Perhaps, if you did start to sing, it would be so loud they
would hear you in the world outside
Perhaps it will be so loud that Richard Russell up there in
his plane
Will hear it crackle on his radio and will decide to keep
flying just a little longer
Just whilst we continue to sing.

Us down here
Him up there

Choosing to continue, despite it all
To start the day as we mean to go on
Together
Singing
Flying

And that would be the end of the show.

And maybe all the audience sing
Or maybe they don't.
But it would be nice if they did.

Singing all together
As the show comes to an end.

End.

Appendix I: Postcards from a Victory Lap

I spent a long time looking at the landscape of the Washington coast, over which Richard flew during his final flight. Below are some excerpts of images I liked, documenting Olympic National Park and points along the Salish Sea.

1. Airport

2. Island

3. Lighthouse

4. Mountains

5. Olympic National Park

6. Olympic Park

Appendix II

It would be remiss of me to not mention the various texts, albums and pieces that influenced and inspired this one. Authorship is a collaborative process with such influences, so I shall recognise them as such.

The Rings of Saturn by W.G. Sebald

A Visit from the Goon Squad by Jennifer Egan

Flights by Olga Tokarczuk

SINNER GET READY by Lingua Ignota

Futurability: The Age of Impotence and the Horizon of Possibility by Franco 'Bifo' Berardi

Fossil Capital by Andreas Malm

Ghosts of the Near Future by Emma & PJ

Landscape (1989) by Emergency Chorus

The Origin of Capitalism by Ellen Meiksins Wood

For a complete listing of
Methuen Drama titles, visit:

www.bloomsbury.com/drama

Follow us on Twitter and keep up to date
with our news and publications

@MethuenDrama